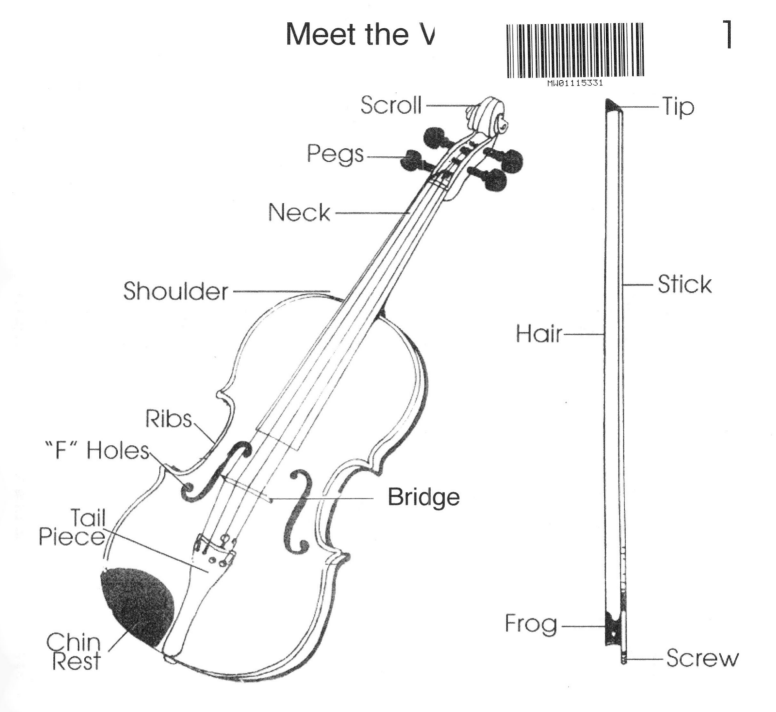

Scroll

Pegs

Neck

Shoulder

Ribs

"F" Holes

Tail Piece

Chin Rest

Bridge

Tip

Stick

Hair

Frog

Screw

Viola Strings

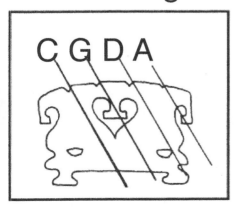

C G D A

Internet Support on the Web

Visit our website for information on the DVD and play-a-long videos.

www.violinfunbook.com

2

Welcome to the wonderful world of viola!

Let's begin with plucking!

My First Song

Notes and Rests

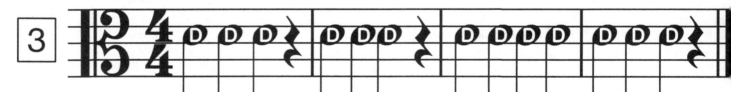

Three's a Crowd

Getting Tricky

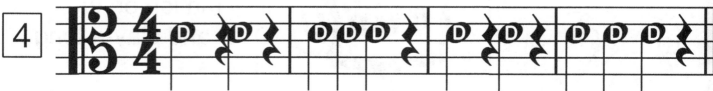

3

A Funny Pair

Zoomin' Along

Skateboard Sam

Let's Play Catch

4

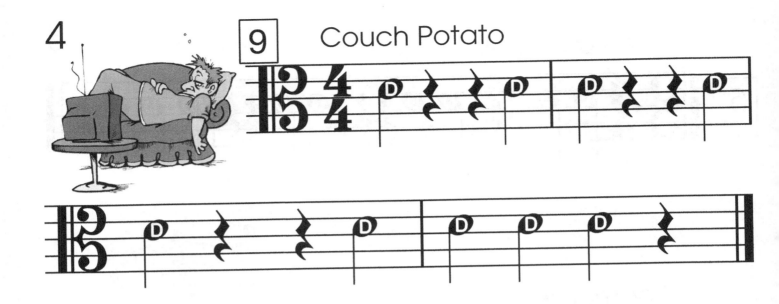

9 Couch Potato

Meet the "A" Team

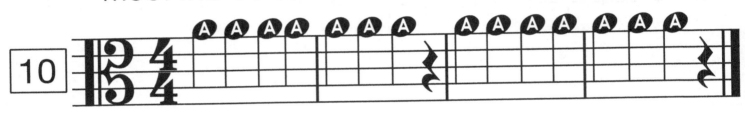

10

11 Puppy Dog Song

Eyes on the Road

12

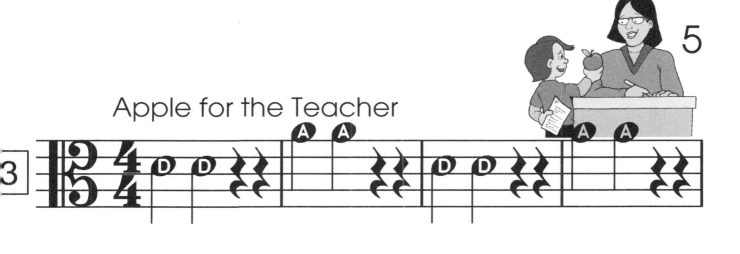

Apple for the Teacher

3

14 Dad's Tune

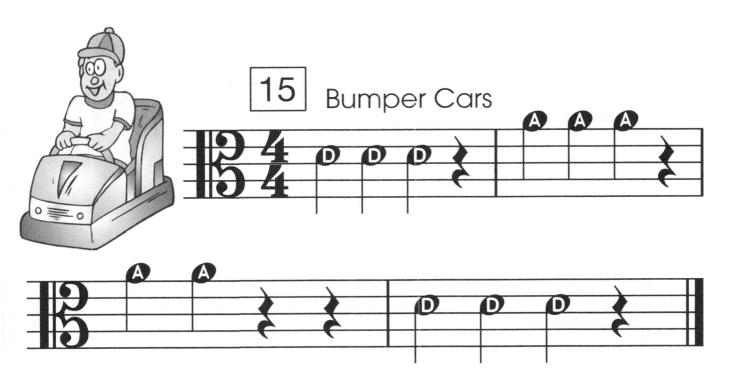

15 Bumper Cars

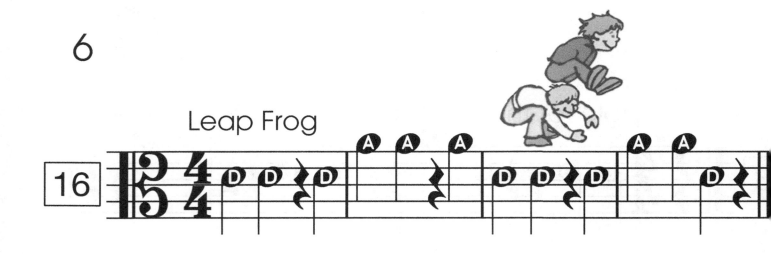

Leap Frog

16

17 Farmer Dave

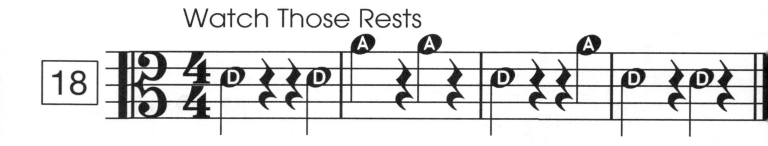

Watch Those Rests

18

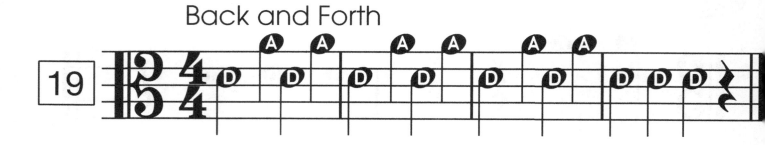

Back and Forth

19

Learning the Bow Grip

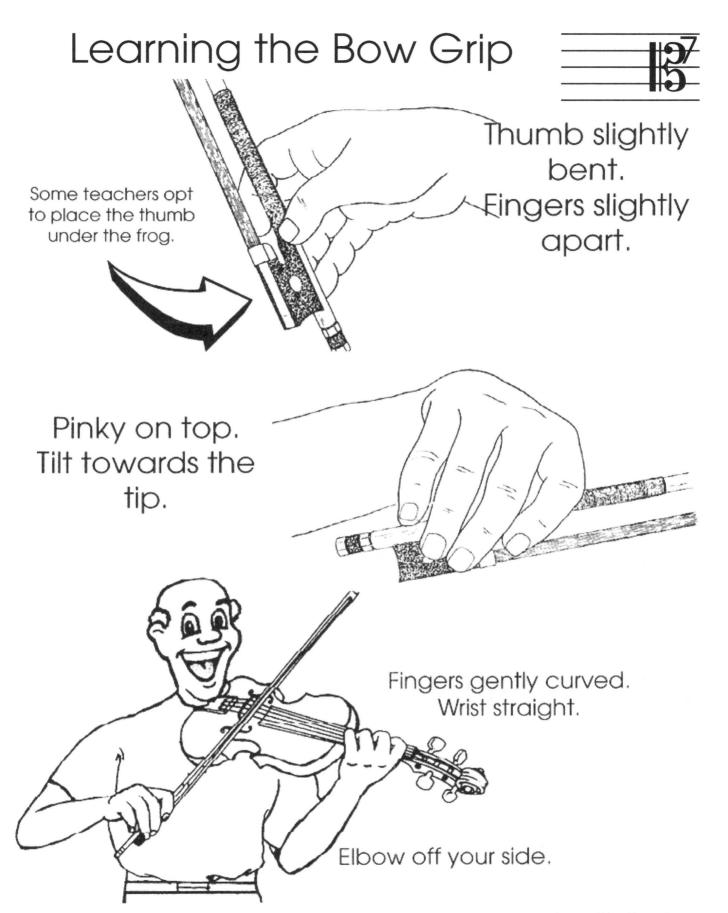

Thumb slightly bent.
Fingers slightly apart.

Some teachers opt to place the thumb under the frog.

Pinky on top. Tilt towards the tip.

Fingers gently curved.
Wrist straight.

Elbow off your side.

Now go back and play the first part of the book again with the bow.

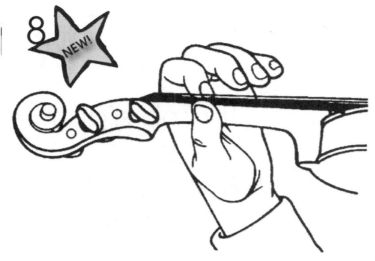

NEW NOTE — First Finger "E"

To play our new note, place the first finger of your left hand down on the "D" string's first tape or mark.

Curve your fingers & use the tip of of your pointer finger on the "D" string.

Relax your thumb.

Press firmly and play the "D" sting with your bow.

My First Finger E

20

The Fabulous Mr. Ed

21

Fun with D and E

22

Banana Split

23

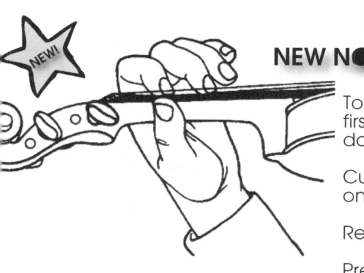

NEW NOTE

To play our new note, place the first and second fingers of your left hand down on the "D" string's first two tapes.

Curve your fingers & use your finger tips on the "D" string.

Relax your thumb.

Press firmly and play the "D" sting with your bow.

Two Fingers Down

Two or Nothing

Trucking Along

Playing It Right

10

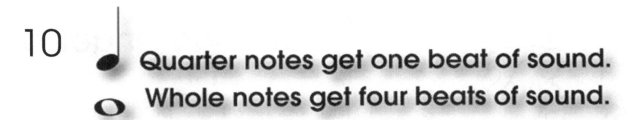

Quarter notes get one beat of sound.
Whole notes get four beats of sound.

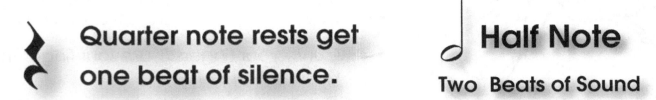

Quarter note rests get one beat of silence.

Half Note

Two Beats of Sound

Half Notes Happen

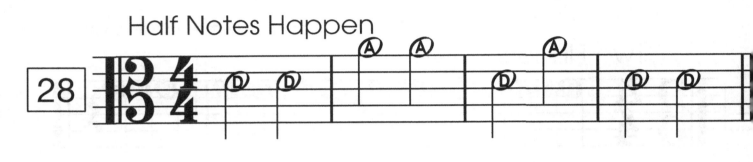

Ups and Downs

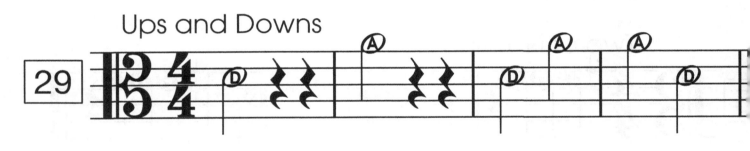

30 Hot Cross Buns

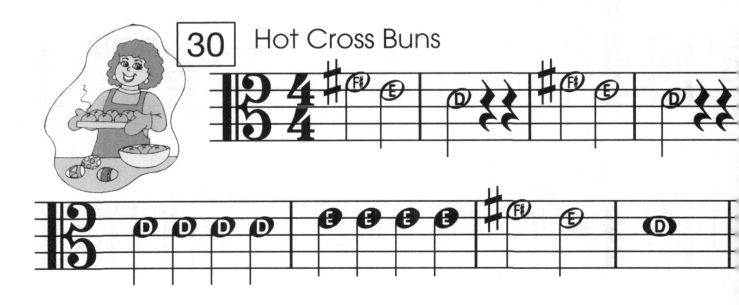

Time Signature

When you see this time signature, you have four beats in each measure.

Mary Had A Little Lamb

12

The Ballerinas

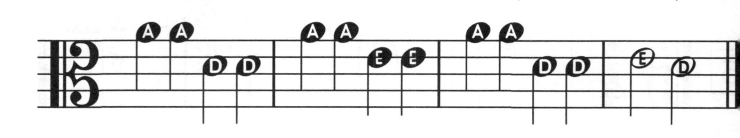

36

The Boy Scout

37

NEW NOTE

Third Finger "G"

To play our new note, place the first, second and third fingers of your left hand down on the "D" string's first three tapes.

Curve your fingers & use your finger tips on the "D" string.

Relax your thumb.

Press firmly and play the "D" sting with your bow.

Give Me A "G"

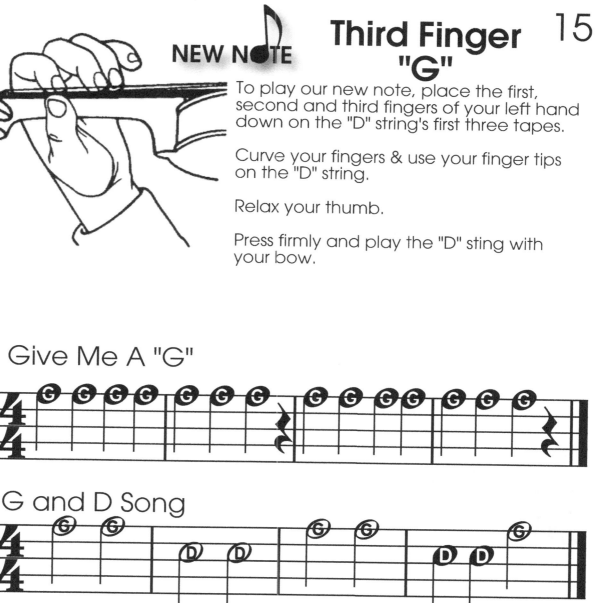

G and D Song

Movin' On Up

Skipin' Town

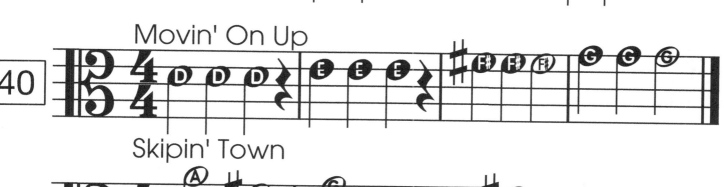

Lightly Row

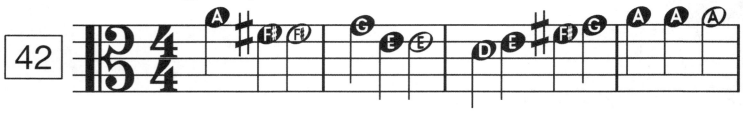

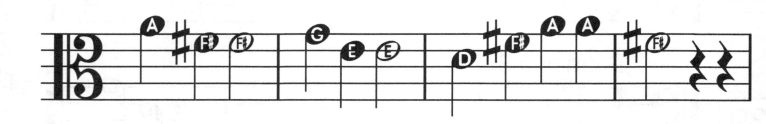

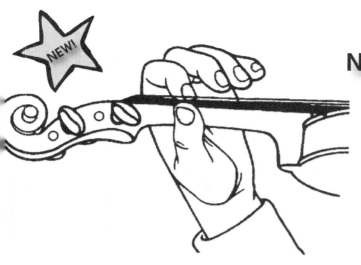

First Finger "B"

To play our new note, place the first finger of your left hand down on the "A" string's first tape or mark.

Curve your fingers & use the tip of of your pointer finger on the "A" string.

Relax your thumb.

Press firmly and play the "A" sting with your bow.

Better "B" Good

"A" vs. "B"

Song Without Letters

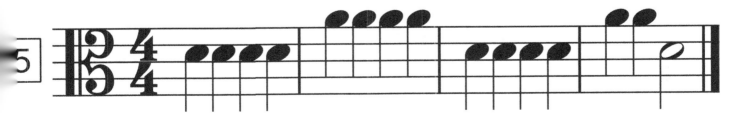

18

Twinkle, Twinkle, Little Star

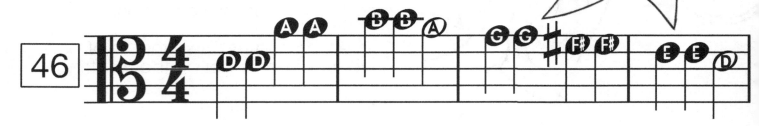

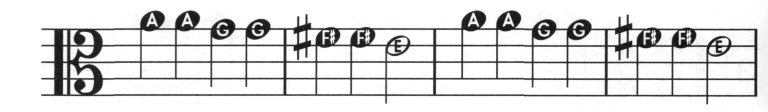

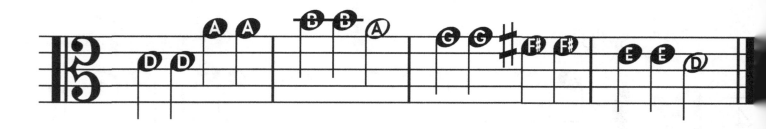

Fun Work   Name the notes.

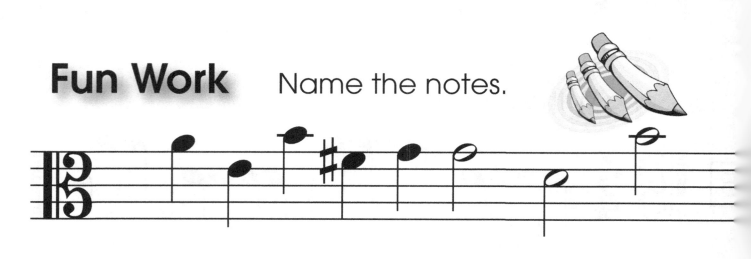

DOWN BOW

Move the bow away from your body (to the right) for a DOWN bow.

UP BOW

Move the bow toward your body (to the left) for an UP bow.

Down and Up

47

Love My Bow

48

Bow Time

49

Jingle Bells

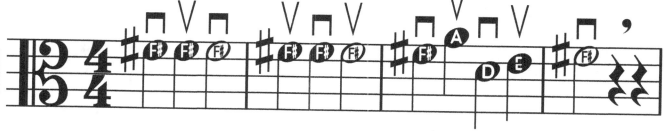

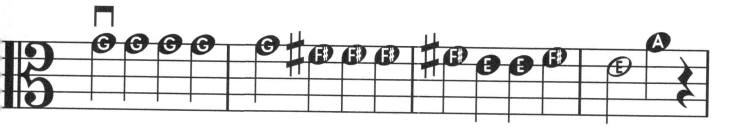

Repeat Sign

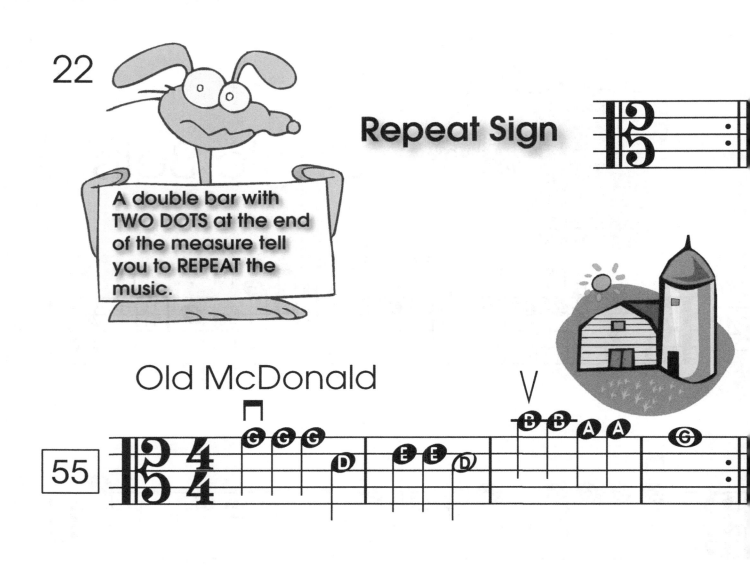

A double bar with TWO DOTS at the end of the measure tell you to REPEAT the music.

Old McDonald

55

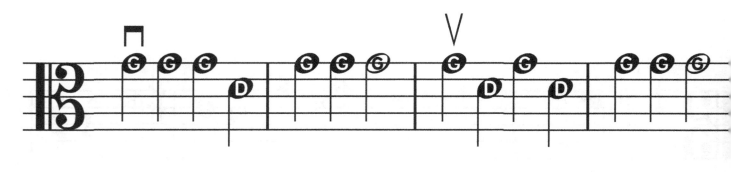

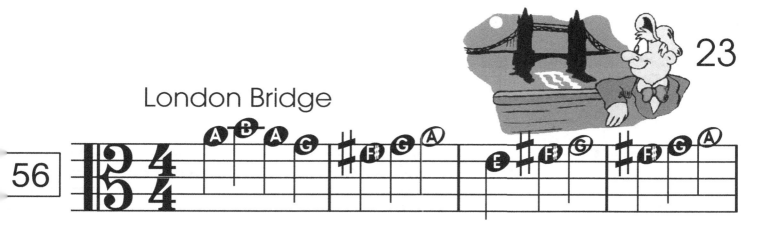

London Bridge

56

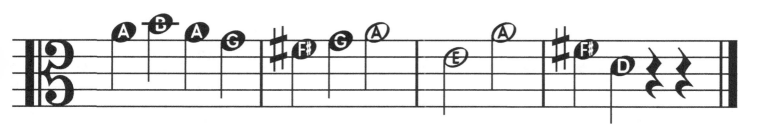

NEW!

A dotted half note gets three beats of sound.

Three Counts Each

57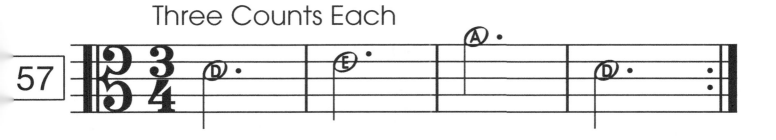

Careful Counter

58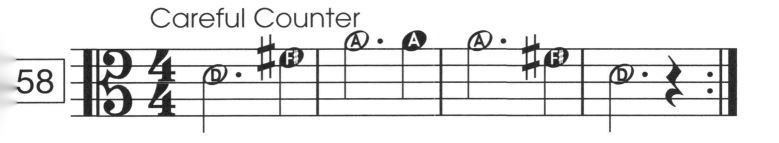

59 Hey, Diddle, Diddle

60 Cukoo Bird

NEW NOTE

"C#"

To play our new note, place the first and second fingers of your left hand down on the "A" string's first two tapes.

Curve your fingers & use your finger tips on the "A" string.

Relax your thumb.

Press firmly and play the "A" sting with your bow.

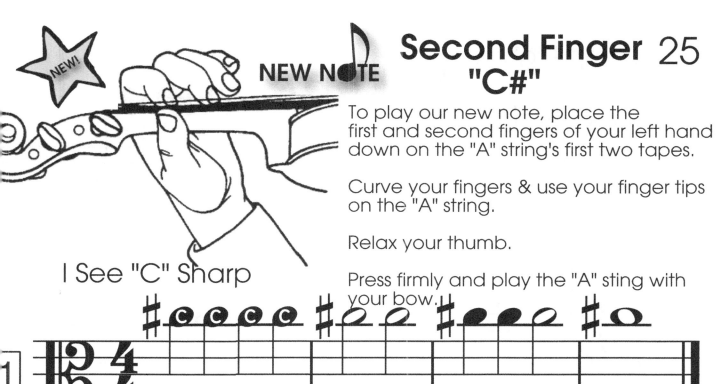

I See "C" Sharp

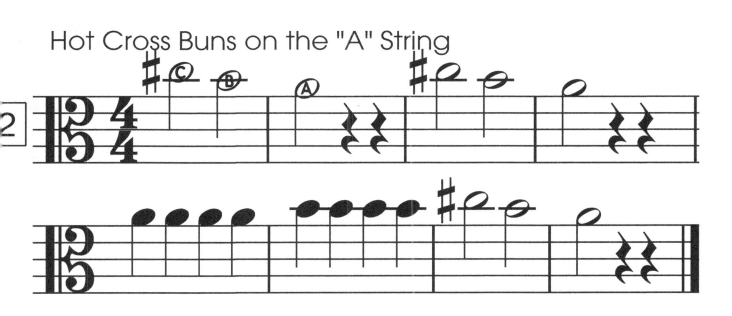

Hot Cross Buns on the "A" String

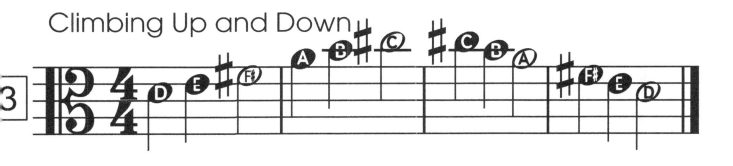

Climbing Up and Down

26 Jump Right In

We Can All Read!

Fun Work Name the notes written on the staff below.

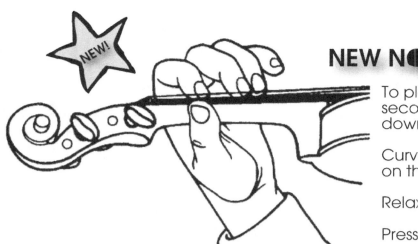

NEW NOTE

Third Finger "D"

To play our new note, place the first, second and third fingers of your left hand down on the "A" string's first three tapes.

Curve your fingers & use your finger tips on the "A" string.

Relax your thumb.

Press firmly and play the "D" sting with your bow.

Meet the Mr. "D"

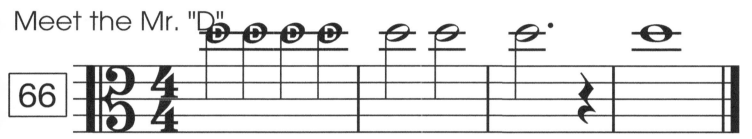

My Sombrero

The Eagle Waltz

Pencil and Eraser Waltz

70 Buffalo Gals

Tie

A "tie" is a curved line that connects two or more notes of the same pitch.

Hold the note for the combined value of the notes.

Tied Score

1

TIE   TIE   TIE

Looby Loo

2

30

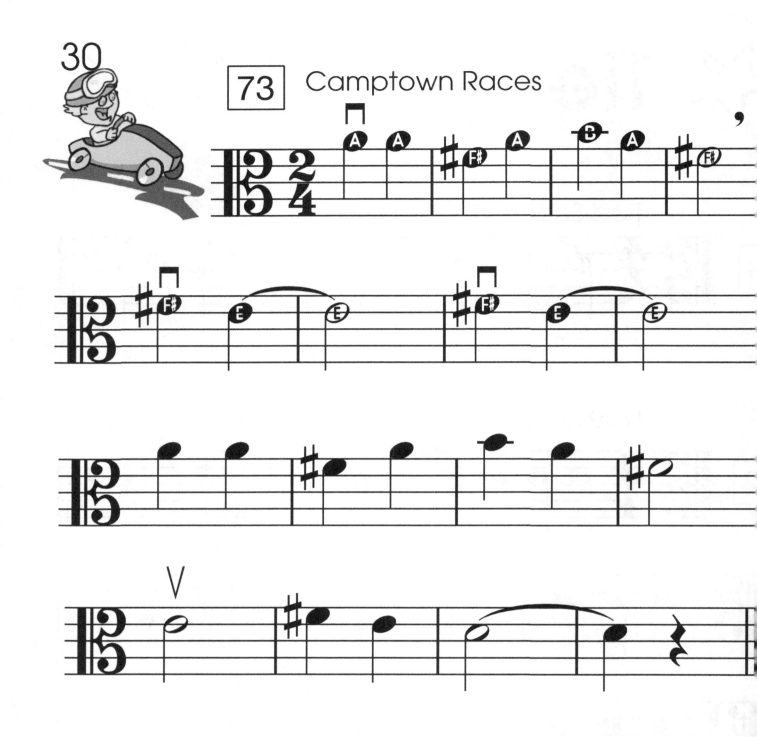

73 Camptown Races

Fun Work

Draw the notes on the staff.

A - D - E - G - F# - B

To play our new note, raise your right elbow slightly and play your open "G" string..

Open "G" is below the music staff.

My Low, Fat "G"

74

Grandma's Tune

75

Mama's Little Baby Loves
Shortnin' Bread

Pop Corn

Oh Susannah

Eighth Notes

One eighth note gets 1/2 count.
Two eighth notes get ONE count.

Dynamics

 _p_   Piano   Play with a soft volume.

 _f_   Forte   Play with a loud volume.

Cabbage Song

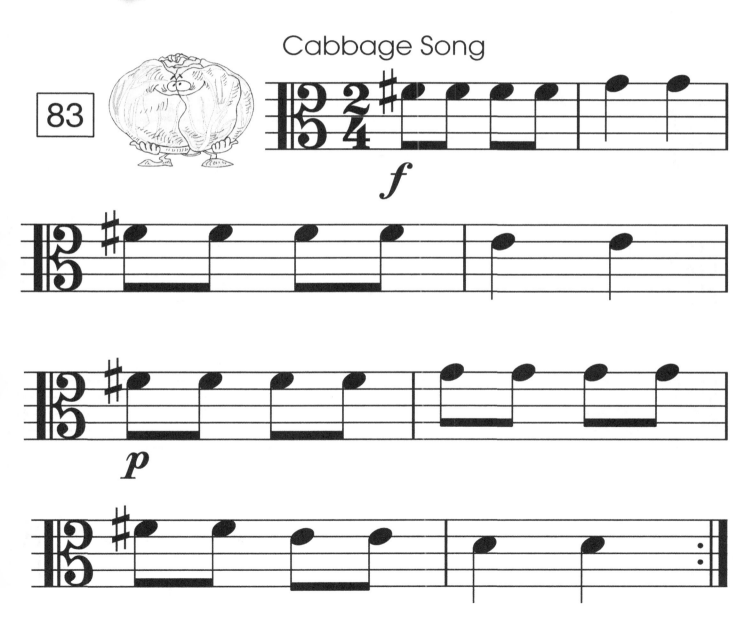

36

Humpty Dumpty

Slur

A SLUR is a curved line that connects two notes of different pitches.

Move you bow in the same direction for the slurred notes. Don't stop the bow. Use an equal amount of bow for each note in the slur.

Slippery Slurs

My Dog and Me

Clowns of Paris

Ode to Joy

40

Good King Wenceslas

Aura Lee

Frog Song

Dreydl, Dreydl

Jolly Old St. Nicholas

42

The Bridge at Avignon

Pop Goes the Weasel

Are You Sleeping?

Musette

Lo Yisa Goy

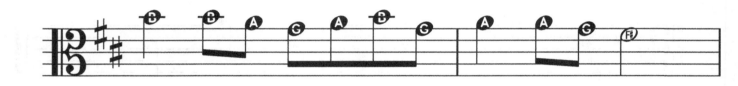

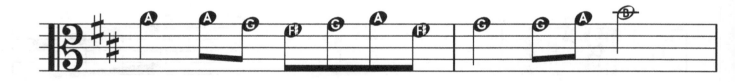

Symphony No.1 by Brahms

This Little Light of Mine

101 Up on the House Top

102 This Old Man

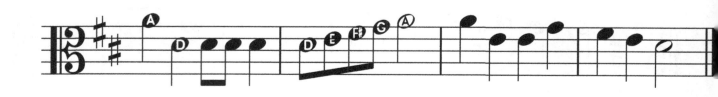

Largo from New World Symphony

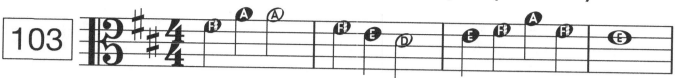

103

Kum Ba Yah

104

Shepherd's Hey

105

Name the Parts

Name the Strings

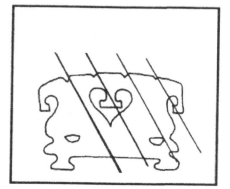

Matching Game

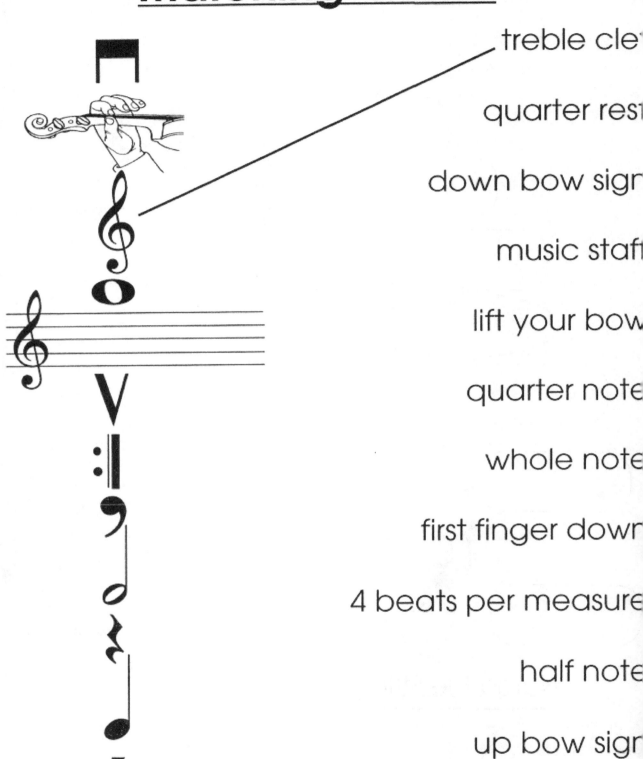

treble clef

quarter rest

down bow sign

music staff

lift your bow

quarter note

whole note

first finger down

4 beats per measure

half note

up bow sign

repeat sign

Violin

Y is for Violin

Violin

Violin

Cello

Bass

Flute

saxophone

Trumpet

French Horn

Trombone

Tuba

Congos

Guitar

Piano

Made in the USA
Las Vegas, NV
02 October 2023